LEARN TO DRAW

Disney PRINCESS

Enchanted Princesses

Learn to draw Ariel, Cinderella, Belle, Rapunzel, and all of your favorite Disney princesses!

Illustrated by The Disney Storybook Artists

WalterFoster

Table of Contents

Tools & Materials

You'll need only a few supplies to create all of your favorite Disney princesses. You may prefer working with a drawing pencil to begin with, and it's always a good idea to have a pencil sharpener and an eraser nearby. When you've finished drawing, you can add color with felt-tip markers, colored pencils, watercolors, or acrylic paint. The choice is yours!

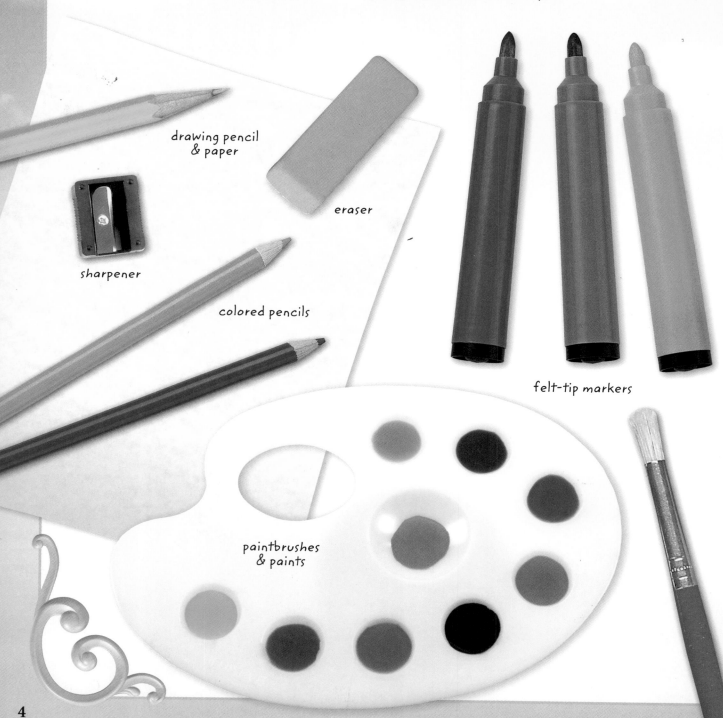

drawing pencil
& paper

eraser

sharpener

colored pencils

felt-tip markers

paintbrushes
& paints

How to Use This Book

In this book you'll learn to draw your favorite princesses in just a few simple steps. You'll also get lots of helpful tips and useful information from Disney artists that will guide you through the drawing process. With a little practice, you'll soon be producing successful drawings of your own!

First draw the basic shapes using light lines that will be easy to erase.

Each new step is shown in blue, so you'll know what to draw next.

Follow the blue lines to draw the details.

Now darken the lines you want to keep, and erase the rest.

Use some magic (or crayons or markers) to add color to your drawing!

Drawing Exercises

Warm up your hand by drawing squiggles and shapes on a piece of scrap paper.

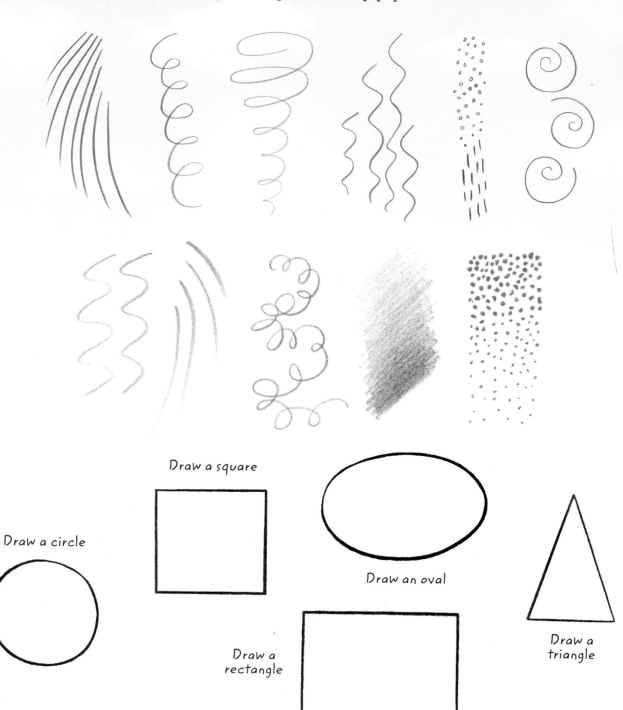

Draw a square

Draw a circle

Draw an oval

Draw a rectangle

Draw a triangle

If you can draw a few basic shapes, you can draw just about anything!

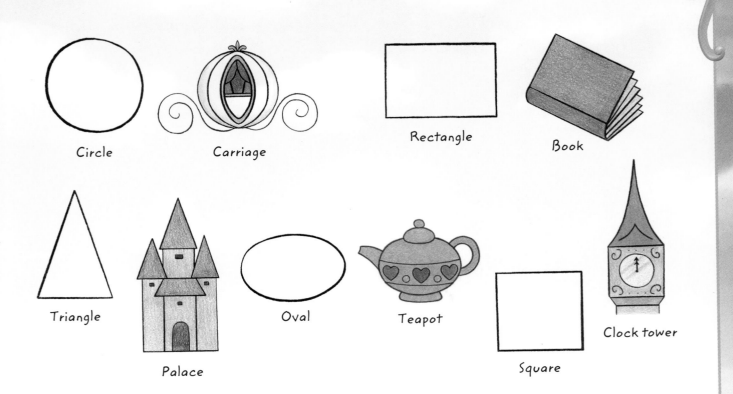

Circle   Carriage   Rectangle   Book

Triangle   Palace   Oval   Teapot   Square   Clock tower

Look how you can turn your doodles into drawings!

Butterfly   Tiara   Balloon

Gown   Bird

Snow White

Snow White is a beautiful young princess who is badly mistreated by her wicked stepmother, the Queen. When creating Snow White, Walt Disney decided to make his first feature princess look more like a pretty "girl next door" than like a glamorous princess. Snow White does have rose-red lips, ebony hair, and skin as white as snow that win her the title of "fairest one of all." But her rounded face and figure also show her youth and innocence.

Snow White's hair is drawn with soft curves

eyelashes curl out from her eyelids

top lip is thinner than bottom lip

NO! bridge of
Snow White's
nose not seen
unless in profile
(side view)

lips are
soft and
not too full

3

1

3/4

1/2

1/4

0

Snow White's
features follow
these guidelines

4

5

Snow White

Even when she's abandoned in the forest, Snow White's kindness shines through and wins her the friendship of all the forest animals—as well as the love and loyalty of the Seven Dwarfs. When you draw Snow White, be sure to show the soft, sweeping lines in her dress and the gentle arm movements that emphasize her cheerful, sweet disposition and her joy for life.

NO! not too curvy

lines are graceful

NO! not angular

Snow White
is about 6
heads tall

figure is
rounded

5

6

hands are rounded
and soft . . .

. . . not sharp
and pointed

draw the legs
as a guide, even
though they're
covered by
skirt

YES! skirt is
wider than
hips

feet are small
and delicate

Cinderella

Cinderella's story seems much like Snow White's at first. She is treated badly by her stepfamily, but she overcomes all to win the love of a prince. She is also as pretty as can be, whether she appears as a simple house maiden with her hair pulled back or as a glamorous ball guest with her hair swept up.

Cinderella has almond-shaped eyes

YES! eyelids have slight S-curve

NO! not droopy— avoid sad eyes

YES! just slight
suggestion of nose

NO! nose is not a
full shape

Cinderella

Cinderella's beauty and graceful movements are evident as she runs down the stairs in her simple, homemade gown, but they are even more obvious at the ball. When she first arrives in her gorgeous dress (thanks to her Fairy Godmother), she immediately attracts everyone's attention, including Prince Charming's. When you draw her sweeping gown with billowing curves, show just a bit of the elegant lace underneath.

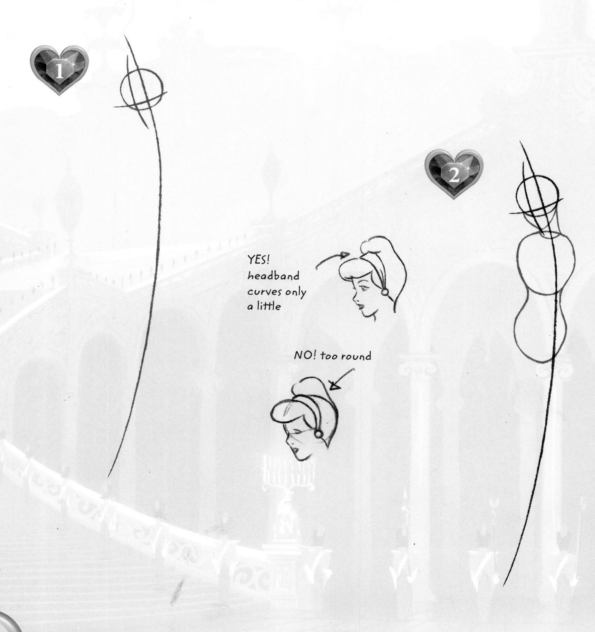

YES! headband curves only a little

NO! too round

3

Cinderella is about 6-1/2 heads tall

4

YES! Cinderella's waist is full but not too plump

NO! waist is not so thin

headband is straighter on top than on side

Cinderella's fingers are long and slender

YES! angles are soft and smooth

NO! angles are not sharp

Sleeping Beauty

When Aurora is awakened from her sleep by a kiss from Prince Phillip, she is saved from the curse placed upon her at birth—and she gets to marry her true love! Now when she dances with her prince in the palace, her simple dress is exchanged for a lovely gown, and a beautiful tiara replaces her plain headband. Use long, slightly curved lines for her skirt to show how regal this princess has become.

eyes tilt up slightly

3

top of head is fairly flat

Sleeping Beauty's features are more angular than Snow White's or Cinderella's

4

YES! eyes end in pointed corners and have one thick eyelash

NO! not round— don't draw individual lashes

Sleeping Beauty
is about 6-1/2
heads tall

waist is
very slim

Sleeping Beauty's
hair curls like this
at the back

YES! Sleeping Beauty's hair extends behind head at an angle

NO! not straight down the back of head

large bangs on left

big curl on right

YES! curls are closed, like this

NO! not open curls

when she dances, hair swings out like this

Ariel

Ariel presents a fun challenge to draw because she can be drawn both in the water
and on land. Whether wearing a ball gown or swimming like a fish,
Ariel is always playful and elegant.

YES! Ariel's
bangs poof
out over her
forehead

NO! hair
doesn't
cover face

YES! Ariel's eyes are
wedge-shaped

NO!
not triangular . . .

. . . nor round

YES! lips are
smooth curves

NO! there's no
"dimple" on
top lip

hair billows
out, especially
underwater

each eyebrow is one thin line

YES! thin eyebrows

NO! not thick

YES! oval nose is angled like this

NO! not horizontal like this

Ariel

People around the world have been charmed by Ariel's cheerful enthusiasm. Be sure to show some of her energy when drawing her complete figure.

Ariel is about 6-1/2 heads tall from the top of her hair to the tip of her fins

Ariel's body curves more behind . . .

. . . and curves less in front

YES! fin
overlaps

NO! not on
each side
of body

even when
sitting, body
is straighter
here . . .

. . . and more
curved here

tail fin
overlaps
body here

4

5

Ariel's Expressions

Knowing the attitude you would like to portray can make the character more believable. Even though expressions create shape changes in Ariel's face, the head volume remains the same.

determined

daydreaming

enchanted

happy

surprised

concerned

amused

Ariel Action Poses

Ariel's personality, mannerisms, and charm all come to life with the right action poses. Practice drawing the poses illustrated and then create some new ones of your own.

Belle

Belle is a simple country girl, with a natural beauty and inner goodness. In this front view of Belle's head, notice how soft curves create her innocent beauty.

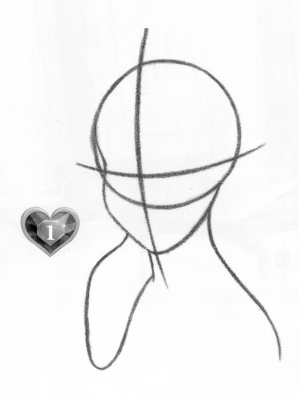

YES! Belle's eyes have slight angles

angle

angle

NO! not smooth oval

Belle has simple features

nose is fairly long with defined bridge

thin upper lip

YES! upper lip is thinner than lower lip

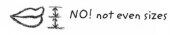

NO! not even sizes

YES! eyebrows
are smooth
and thin

NO! not thick
or angular

1

2/3

1/3

0

Belle's facial features follow
these guidelines

hair bow extends
beyond chin line

3

4

5

when eyes close,
angle of eyes is
less dramatic

Belle

Belle radiates kindness and love in her elegant ball gown.

when worn down, Belle's hair is drawn with simple shapes that wrap around her head

YES! hair curves around head

NO! no straight line across head

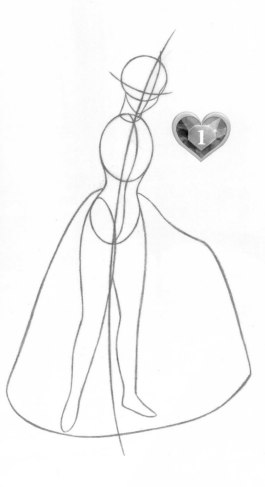

Belle is about 6½ heads tall

in ponytail, hair
is pulled close
to head

Belle's Expressions

Belle's love of books makes her yearn for faraway places and adventures.
Knowing her traits will help you draw Belle in a variety of moods and expressions.

caring

amused

skeptical

happy

surprised

daydreaming

worried

frightened

Belle Action Poses

Now that you've learned to draw Belle's face and body, you can really bring her to life in these action poses.

Jasmine

The beautiful Princess Jasmine captures the heart of Aladdin. When drawing this graceful princess, notice how her large brown eyes have a gentle upward slant.

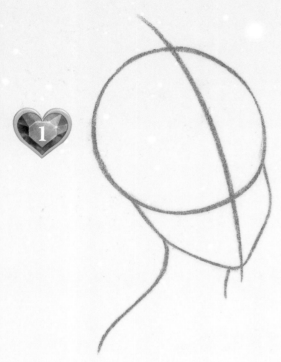

Jasmine has almond-shaped eyes

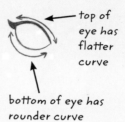

top of eye has flatter curve

bottom of eye has rounder curve

Jasmine's eyes have gentle slant, like cat's eyes

YES! eyes follow bottom of guide-line circle

NO! not straight across face

eyes are about 1 eye-width apart

thick
eyebrows

hair overlaps
eyebrows

full bottom lip

YES! back of hair
comes out to soft
point

NO! not round;
not so small

Jasmine

Jasmine has a slender figure. She carries herself with dignity and grace.

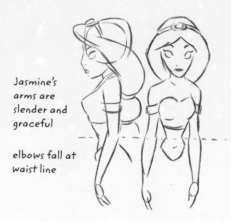

Jasmine's arms are slender and graceful

elbows fall at waist line

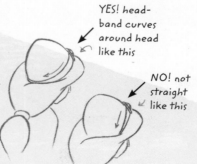

YES! head-band curves around head like this

NO! not straight like this

Jasmine is just a little more than 5 heads tall

Jasmine Action Poses

Jasmine may look delicate, but she is a fiery beauty and can take care of herself.
Enhance her personality with the following mannerisms and poses.

Pocahontas

The beautiful Pocahontas has a strong, noble face with high cheekbones, piercing eyes, and flowing black hair.

The tip of Pocahontas's nose should be very close to her upper lip.

Pocahontas

Pocahontas's body is athletic yet feminine. She stands with her shoulders back and her head held high.

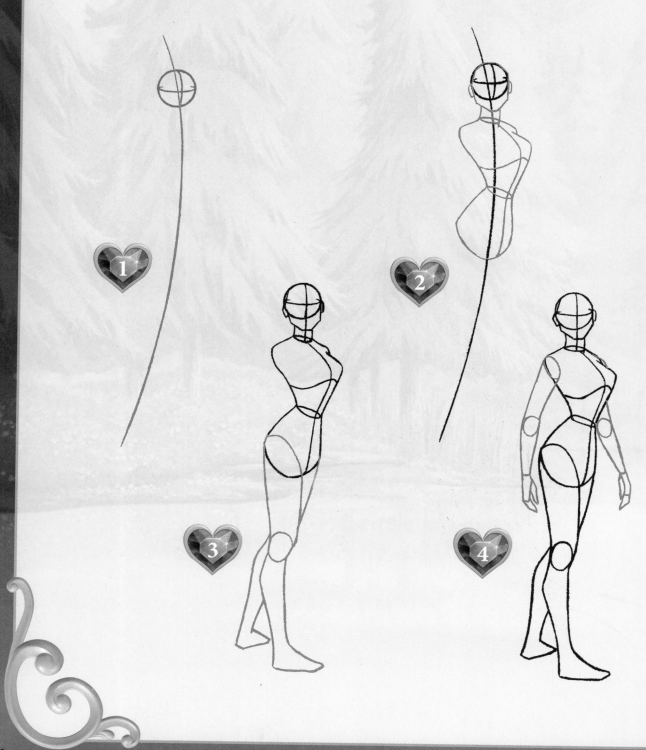

Pocahontas's Expressions

Pocahontas has mixed emotions after the arrival of John Smith and the other settlers.

proud

happy

worried

excited

angry

surprised

pensive

Mulan

This plucky heroine is a study in contrasts. Mulan is graceful, yet feisty; respectful, yet defiant. Behind her classic Asian features lies a quick mind—and she's not afraid to speak it. Animators had to show both the outwardly traditional Mulan and her bold inner spirit. They chose to create her character using simple shapes and few details. Her clean, down-to-earth look emphasizes that she just wants to be true to herself. As you draw Mulan, focus on simplicity, shape, and proportion.

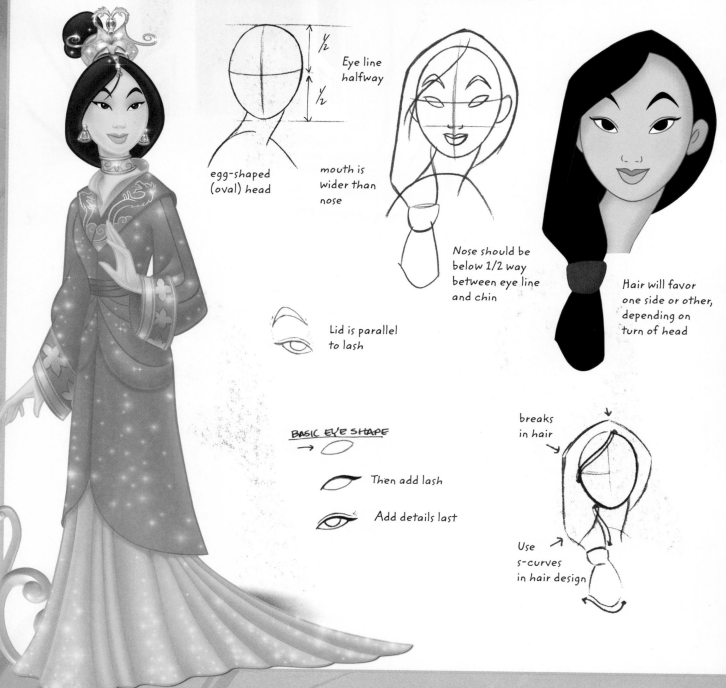

Eye line halfway

$\frac{1}{2}$
$\frac{1}{2}$

egg-shaped (oval) head

mouth is wider than nose

Nose should be below 1/2 way between eye line and chin

Hair will favor one side or other, depending on turn of head

Lid is parallel to lash

BASIC EYE SHAPE

Then add lash

Add details last

breaks in hair

Use s-curves in hair design

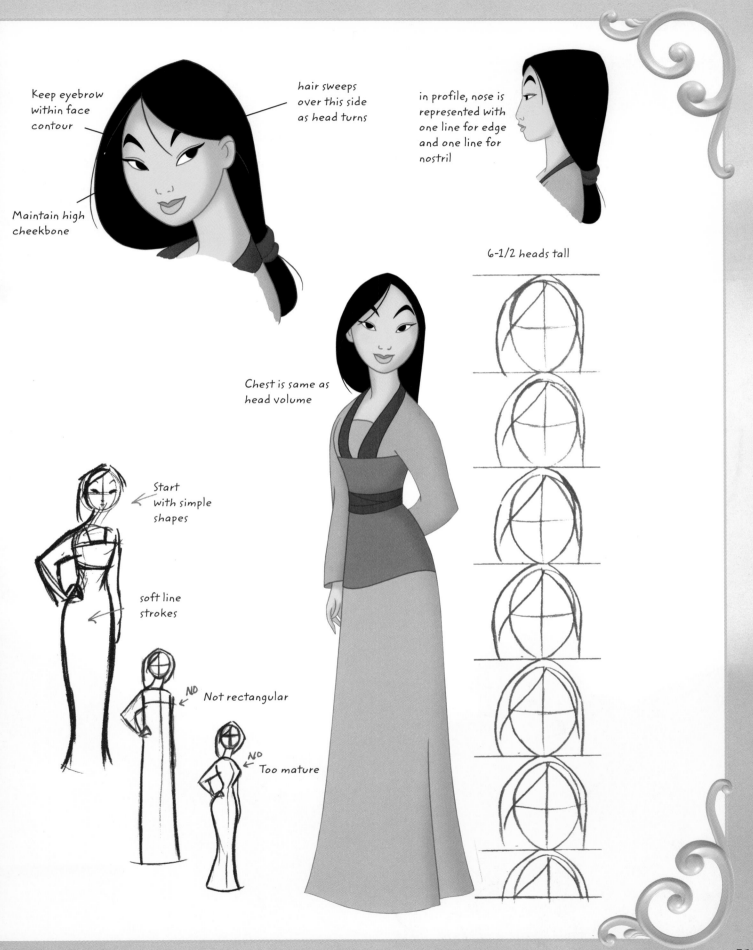

Keep eyebrow within face contour

hair sweeps over this side as head turns

in profile, nose is represented with one line for edge and one line for nostril

Maintain high cheekbone

6-1/2 heads tall

Chest is same as head volume

Start with simple shapes

soft line strokes

NO Not rectangular

NO Too mature

Mulan as Soldier

Mulan becomes a soldier to save her elderly father's life. She defies tradition, doing what she believes is right. The film's artists have followed her daring lead and treated her "soldier" look with an unconventional approach. Her basic features are the same, but slight changes have been made to help hide her femininity. Here are some secrets to drawing Mulan as a soldier:

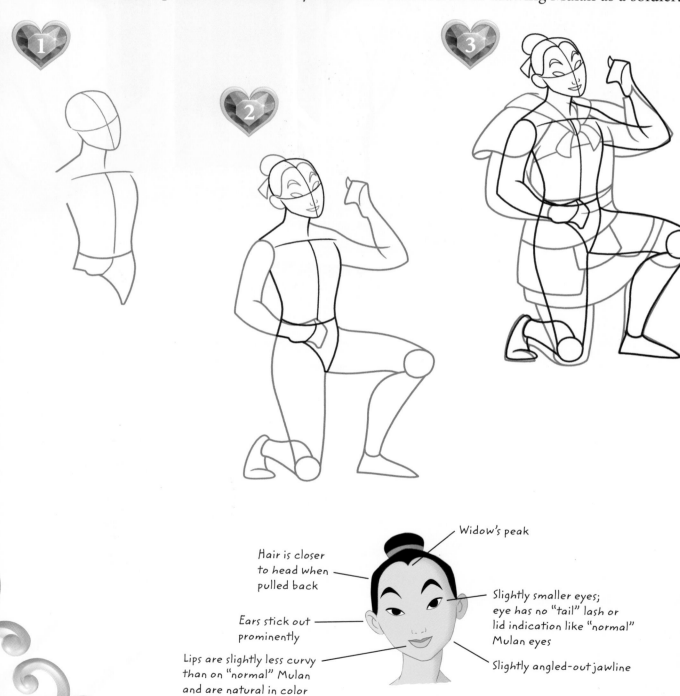

Widow's peak

Hair is closer to head when pulled back

Ears stick out prominently

Lips are slightly less curvy than on "normal" Mulan and are natural in color

Slightly smaller eyes; eye has no "tail" lash or lid indication like "normal" Mulan eyes

Slightly angled-out jawline

4

Even when she is in armor, retain Mulan's graceful shapes

Show some thickness of hair

S-curve shallow bridge

Eye close to nose

slight overbite

5

Watch space here

NO!
Too wide

Too small

Tiana

Tiana grows up to be an intelligent, beautiful, hardworking young woman, and a very talented cook. She works several waitress jobs and saves every penny. Although her friends often invite her out on the town, she always turns them down. Tiana won't stop working until she has enough money to open the restaurant that she and her father had always dreamed of.

head shape
resembles an egg

nose is short
and round

rounded chin

masquerade
ball tiara

YES!
ears are
small and
rounded

NO!
too
pointy

4

5

NO!
too narrow

YES!
large,
rounder
eyes

Tiana

When Tiana marries Naveen, she not only regains her human form, she becomes a princess! Tiana finally gets her dream restaurant and finds true love with her prince!

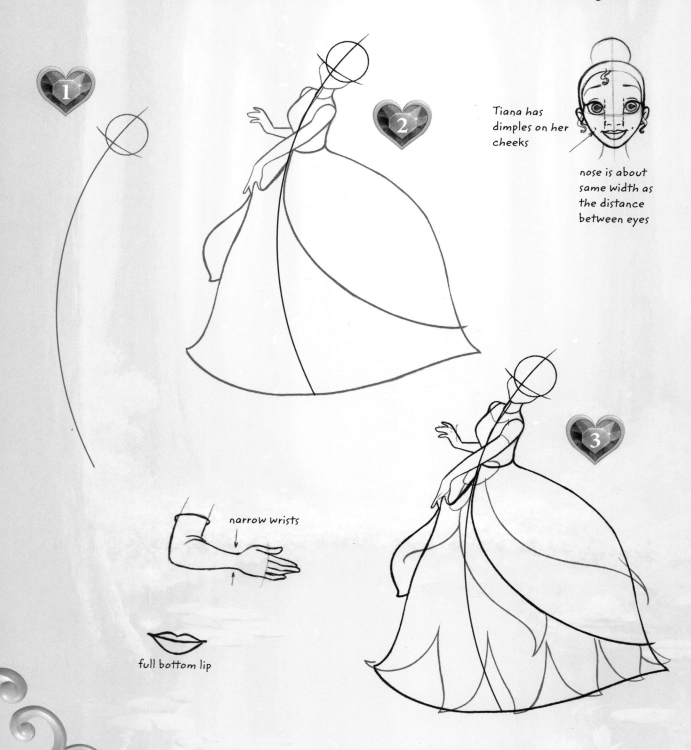

Tiana has dimples on her cheeks

nose is about same width as the distance between eyes

narrow wrists

full bottom lip

Tiana's bayou wedding crown is made of petals and stamens of varying shapes and sizes.

Tiana the Frog

Being green isn't easy! When Tiana is transformed into a frog, she's faced with brand new challenges: finding her way through the bayou, escaping from frog hunters, and catching flies with her long, sticky tongue! But even as a frog, Tiana proves that she's very capable and hardworking. Whether it's making a boat on which to float down the bayou or whipping up a batch of gumbo for her friends, Tiana can get things done.

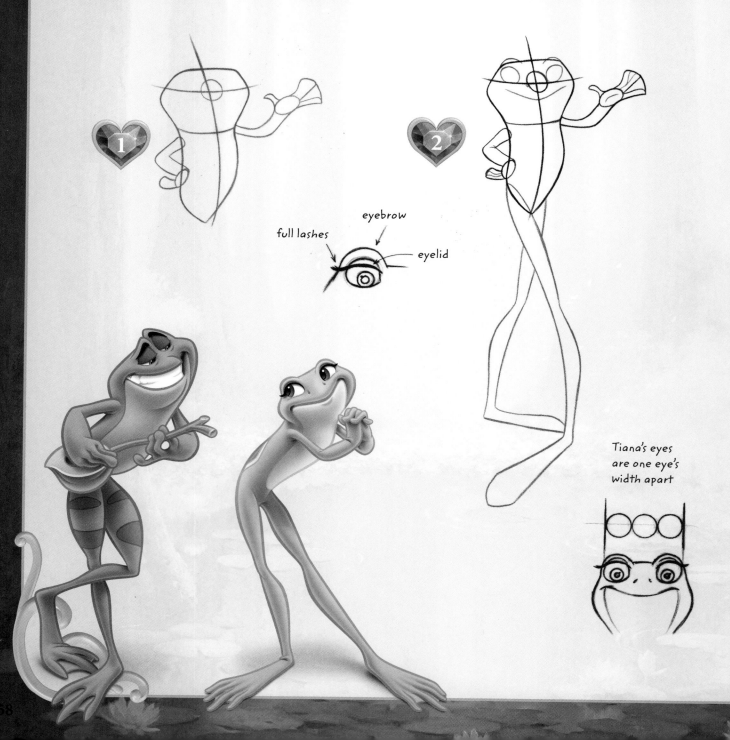

full lashes

eyebrow

eyelid

Tiana's eyes are one eye's width apart

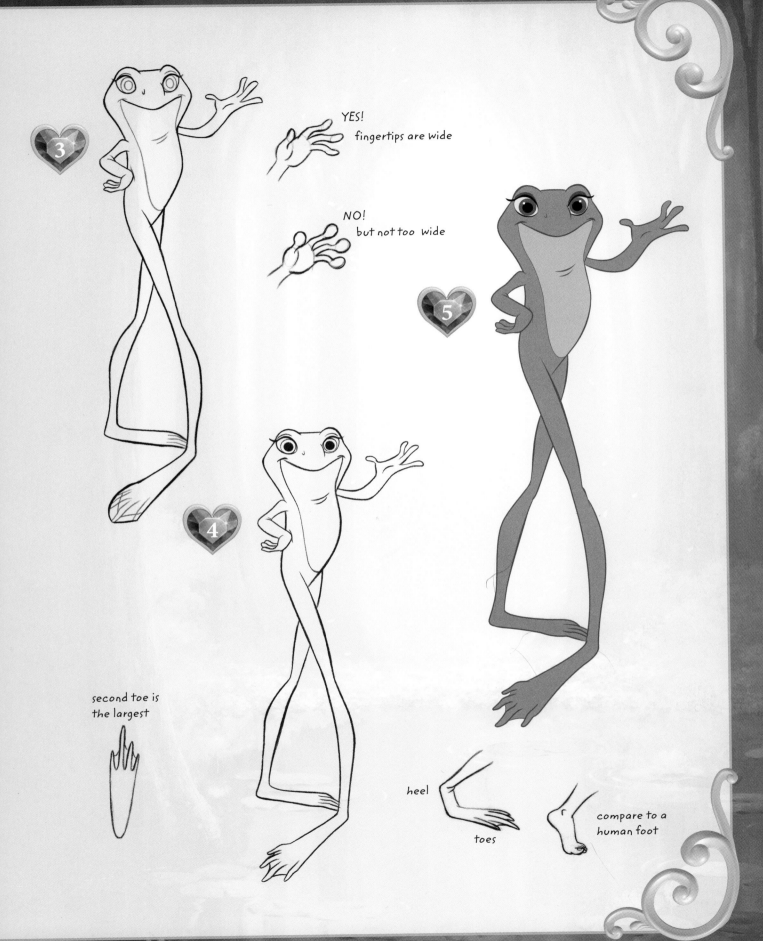

YES!
fingertips are wide

NO!
but not too wide

second toe is
the largest

heel

toes

compare to a
human foot

Rapunzel

Rapunzel may have grown up in a tower, but she is full of energy, which she uses to take care of her hair that grew and grew and grew! Her days are full of many things, including reading, cooking, and painting. Her beautiful art covers the walls (and the ceiling!) of the tower. When drawing Rapunzel, don't forget to think of her spirit and her curiosity about the world outside. Even though she could not leave the tower, she dreamed big!

the "swoop" at the top of Rapunzel's hair is a distinguishing feature of her look

NO!

YES!

hair has volume
and thickness, even when
lying on the floor

Rapunzel's
hair has a lot
of weight that
forms simple
shapes

Rapunzel

Even after Flynn cuts Rapunzel's hair, she remains the spirited young woman she has always been. Being reunited with her parents is a joy, and she cannot believe how amazing the world outside the tower is!

after Rapunzel's hair is cut,
it turns brown and maintains
soft waves along the bottom edges

Conclusion

Now that you've learned the secrets to drawing your favorite Disney princesses, try creating different scenes from the movies, or original scenes of your very own. To create a little magic, all you need is a piece of paper, a pencil, and your imagination!